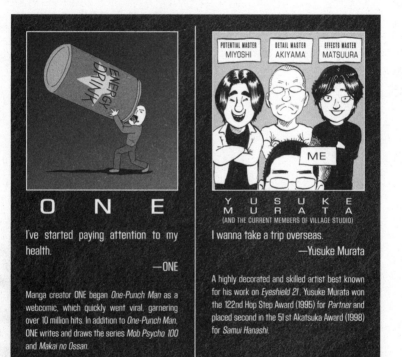

ONE

I've started paying attention to my health.

—ONE

Manga creator ONE began *One-Punch Man* as a webcomic, which quickly went viral, garnering over 10 million hits. In addition to *One-Punch Man*, ONE writes and draws the series *Mob Psycho 100* and *Makai no Ossan*.

YUSUKE MURATA

(AND THE CURRENT MEMBERS OF VILLAGE STUDIO)

I wanna take a trip overseas.

—Yusuke Murata

A highly decorated and skilled artist best known for his work on *Eyeshield 21*, Yusuke Murata won the 122nd Hop Step Award (1995) for *Partner* and placed second in the 51st Akatsuka Award (1998) for *Samui Hanashi*.

ONE-PUNCH MAN 05

ONE + YUSUKE MURATA

★ THE STORIES, CHARACTERS AND INCIDENTS MENTIONED IN THIS PUBLICATION ARE ENTIRELY FICTIONAL.

ONE-PUNCH MAN
05
STORY BY
O N E
ART BY
YUSUKE
MURATA

CHARACTERS

STORY

A single man arose to face the evil threatening humankind!
His name was Saitama. He became a hero for fun!

Together with his pupil Genos, Saitama continues making modest contributions as a Class-C hero. With one punch, he destroys a massive meteor headed for Earth, but no one believes he could be so extraordinarily strong.

Next, the Deep Sea King—leader of the Clan of the Seafolk—attacks! Saitama and Genos race to confront this Demon-level crisis of unprecedented proportions!! The Deep Sea King wanders around destroying the city. In order to save the men he loves, the Class-S hero Puri-Puri Prisoner squares off against this fierce opponent who has easily defeated even Class-A heroes!!

CONTENTS

ONE-PUNCH MAN VOLUME FIVE

ONE-PUNCH MAN

ONE + YUSUKE MURATA

My name is Saitama. I am a hero. My hobby is heroic exploits. I got too strong. And that makes me sad. I can defeat any enemy with one blow. I lost my hair. And I lost all feeling. I want to feel the rush of battle. I would like to meet an incredibly strong enemy. And I would like to defeat it with one blow. That's because I am One-Punch Man.

05

SHINING IN TATTERS

HMM?

ANOTHER FIGHTER?

PUNCH 25: DEEP SEA KING • 2

BOTH STINGER ...

...AND LIGHTNING MAX...

... STRUCK MY FANCY.

I MUST AVENGE THEM!

I'LL START AT *HALF* POWER!

KYAEE!!
I RIPPED MY BOY-FRIEND'S HAND-WOVEN SWEATER!!

KYAA-AAEE-EEEE-EEEE-EEII-IIII-!!!

NOW YOU'VE ***REALLY*** DONE IT!

HUH?

HE'S PRETTY SCARY...

I'M GETTING *SERIOUS*.

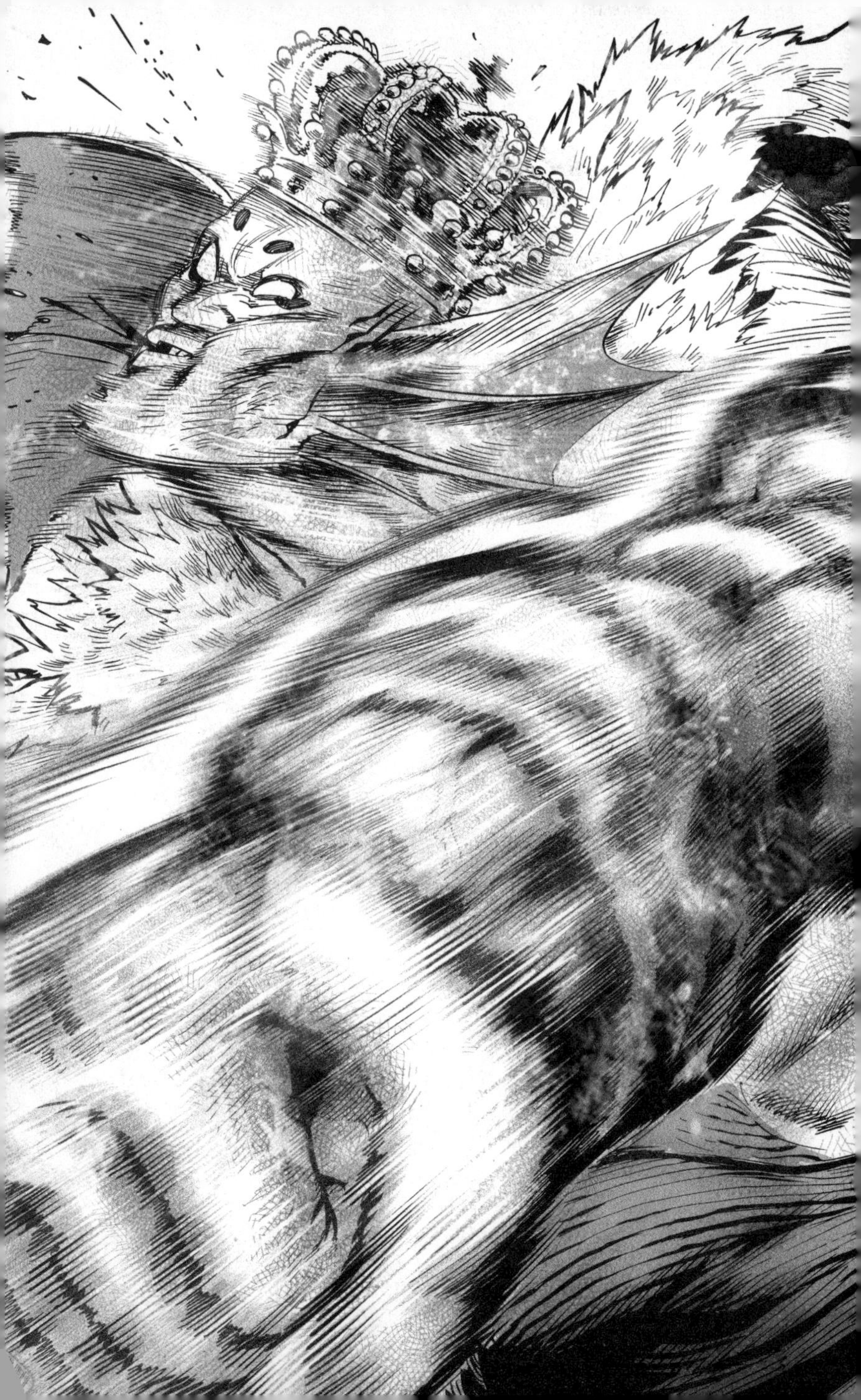

?!

OH MY...

PAW

TMP
DOOOOOM

CRIK CRIK CRIK
I FELT THAT.
A LITTLE.

A SLUGFEST BETWEEN POWERHOUSES... IS THIS WHAT IT'S LIKE WHEN A CLASS-S HERO BATTLES A DEMON-LEVEL CRISIS?
IT'S RIDICU-LOUS...
THERE'S NO WAY I COULD LOSE.

HMF... HE PACKS MORE OF A PUNCH THAN I EXPECTED...
BUT I CAN'T LOSE.
HE MIGHT BEAT UP MORE GUYS!

GUESS I'LL HAVE TO TRANSFORM ...

GET READY FOR THIS!

TRANS-☆FORM!!

BULGE
BULGE
UGH...
HIS MUSCLES EXPANDED, RIPPING OFF HIS CLOTHES. HE'S COMPLETELY NAKED...

THAT'S NO ANGEL... HE'S NOT EVEN HUMAN!

I CAN'T WATCH. I SHOULD LEAVE.

YEAH...
...I REALLY SHOULD LEAVE.

YOU'RE GROSS.

NO ONE WHO SEES MY ANGEL STYLE WALKS AWAY ALIVE!

THOSE WERE YOUR LAST WORDS!

FWEEEE
POW

KR
NK

RRMMMBL
HM?
I GOT SEPA-RATED FROM MASTER ...

DONE WITH YOUR CONSECU-TIVE PUNCHES?

I *DID* FEEL THAT.

A LITTLE.

WHSH
WHUD

SMA
SH
THWOK
CONSECUTIVE PUNCHES...

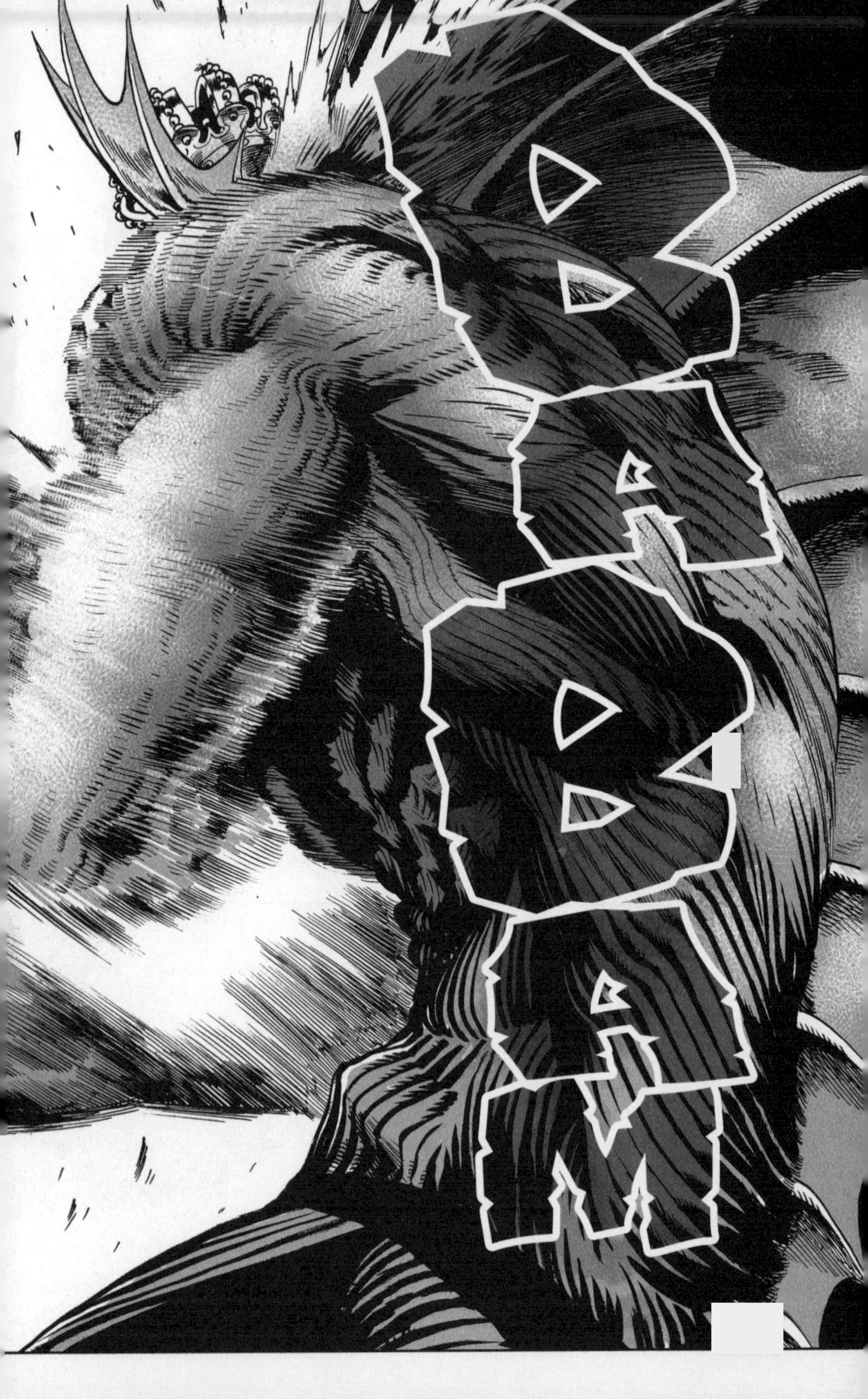
BABAM

SHF

WHAAM

CRASH

THAT WAS FUN!
WHO ARE YOU?

I'M THE *DEEP SEA KING.*

AS LEADER OF THE CLAN OF THE SEAFOLK, I RULE THE DEEP SEA!
AND NOW I RULE *HERE.*
YOU WANNA OPPOSE ME?

HEH...
YOU THINK YOU CAN RULE THE SURFACE ALONE?
BUT YOU COULD LIVE QUIETLY AT THE BOTTOM OF THE SEA. POOR FOOL...

IT'S
RAINING.

PLIP
PLIP

SW
SH
TOO SLOW.

SHWACK
WIND BLADE KICK!!!
DEEP SEA KING, I'M ON TO YOUR MOVES!
I CAN'T LOSE TO YOU!

OH YOU ARE, HUH?
SHASH

TCH!
TOMP
ONCE MY INTERNAL MORAYS BITE YOU ...
...THEY NEVER LET GO!
SHREEEEEEEE

SNAP
GLARE
HM ?!
I'LL SAY THIS AGAIN ...
I CAN'T LOSE TO YOU.

WSH
WHSH
WSH WSH
WHSH
SWOOSH
IT'S NO USE.

YOU HAVE POWER...

...BUT YOU'RE TOO SLOW FOR ME.

I'M SO HAPPY, DEEP SEA KING!

ZOOM

I CAN TEST MY MOVES AGAINST SOMEONE LIKE YOU!

WHAM
BAM
THWAM
POW
I KNEW IT! MY MOVES ARE THE FASTEST AND STRONGEST!!!
HEE HEE!
WEE HEE HEE HEE HEE HEE HEE HEE HEE HEE HEE HEE HEE HEE HEE HEE!
HAVE YOU GONE CRAZY?

!
HE'S FAST!!

?!!
AND HUGE!!

HE'S BIG AND FAST...
BUT I'M FASTER.
GOOM
!
HE JUST GOT EVEN MORE POWER-FUL!!

TOMP
KRMBL KRMBL KRMBL

WHAT HAPPENED ?!

KWOMP
KRAK
!
I REALLY SHRIVELED WHEN I CAME TO THE SURFACE...
GRRR...
...BUT THANKS TO THE RAIN, I'M FEELING BETTER.

YOUR ATTACKS DON'T HURT AT ALL.
HE'S FAST ...
... BIG ...
...AND STRONG ...
...BUT SURELY I CAN'T LOSE...

THE PRESENT LOCATION OF INVADERS FROM THE CLAN OF THE SEAFOLK REMAINS UNKNOWN.

TSHHHHHHH

THE BODIES OF SEVERAL HEROES HAVE BEEN DISCOVERED AT THE SCENE OF THE FIGHT.

THEY ARE SEVERELY INJURED AND UNCONSCIOUS.

THE CORPSES OF SEVERAL MONSTERS THOUGHT SLAIN BY HEROES WERE FOUND...
...BUT DAMAGE TO THE CITY CONTINUES, SO MORE MUST BE ON THE LOOSE.

OUR GUEST TODAY IS THE CLASS-A, RANK-1 SUPERHERO WHO HAS TOPPED THE POPULARITY RANKING FOR 28 WEEKS.

HE'S AN ACTIVE MODEL, ACTOR AND SINGER.

I'M PLEASED TO BE HERE!

THE INVASION HAS REACHED THREAT LEVEL DEMON.

AS A HERO, WHAT'S YOUR TAKE ON THIS INCIDENT?

THAT'S A DIFFICULT QUESTION ...

I'M ONLY A HERO WHEN FACING EVIL.

OTHER TIMES, I'M AN ACTOR, MODEL AND SINGER.

TODAY, I'M HERE TO PROMOTE MY NEW SINGLE, SO...

OH, PARDON ME.

TO CALM THE POPULACE'S UNEASE...

...A HERO MUST BE TOUGH, STRONG AND BEAUTIFUL...

...AS WELL AS ABLE TO PROMPTLY AND SPLENDIDLY ERADICATE EVIL.

IT IS REGRETTABLE THAT SOME HEROES HAVE SUFFERED A CRUSHING DEFEAT...
WHAM
...BUT WE MUST ALL IMPROVE OURSELVES SO THAT NO MORE DIE IN VAIN.
THOOM
KRAASH
URGH!
MY THRUSTS AND KICKS DON'T WORK! DO I LACK POWER ?!

I CAN'T KILL HIM WITH-OUT A WEAPON!
I'LL RETREAT AND GO GET ONE!
GRAB
!!
KRAK
SNAP
POP
KRAK SNAP POP?
?

HUH?
RMMBL...
TSSHHHHH
WAIT RIGHT THERE.
THE NEXT TIME WE MEET, YOU'RE DEAD.
SHOOM

HE'S GONE ...
OH WELL. LET THE LITTLE FISH GO.
NOW ...
...I CAN CONTINUE ON MY WAY!
CLOMP

!

WHO ARE YOU?
WHAT ARE YOU DOING HERE?
?!

DID YOU NOT HEAR THE EVACUATION ALERT?
...
YOU ...

HEH!
A HERO?

DON'T BOTHER TRYING TO DEFEAT THE DEEP SEA KING.
DEEP SEA KING?
EVEN IN A GROUP, YOU HEROES CAN'T WIN.
VWSH
JERKS WHO PLAY AT JUSTICE CAN'T BEAT A REALLY TOUGH OPPONENT.
YOU CAN'T PROTECT ANYTHING!
VOOSH

BEEP

MULTIPLE LIFE-FORMS DETECTED IN THE VICINITY!

SEA-FOLK? AND AT A PLACE NEAR HERE.

IT APPEARS TO BE...

SKLRF

...THE DISASTER EVACUATION SHELTER!

MMMMMMR
PAPA!
ARE THERE STILL SCARY MONSTERS OUTSIDE?
GAKI
DON'T WORRY!
SOMEONE WILL DEFEAT THEM!
OYAJI

CHATTER CHATTER
AND WE'RE SAFE IN THIS SHELTER!
BESIDES, THE FIVE THOUSAND PEOPLE HERE CAN BEAT ONE MONSTER!

I SENSE SOMETHING ...

MANY PRESENCES ...
CLOMP
...OVER THERE.

WHAM
?!
VIP...
!!
EEK!

KRASSH

KRMBL
KRMBL
KRMBL

NICE TO MEET YOU!

AND GOOD-BYE!

PLEASE!

Class-C Hero:

ALLBACK-MAN

IT'S PITIFUL, BUT I SHOULD STALL UNTIL CLASS-S AND CLASS-A GUYS ARRIVE.

OR SHOULD I JOIN ARMS WITH THE MEN HERE?

NO. THIS MONSTER BROKE INTO A MISSILE-PROOF SHELTER.

HOW CAN I BUY TIME? HE'S GOING TO ATTACK ANY SECOND!

OOPS...
I PEED MY PANTS...
I'M SO PITIFUL...

IT'S NO USE. HE'S GOING TO ATTACK!
I CAN'T BUY TIME TALKING.

SHOULD I FIGHT?
SHOULD I FIGHT ?!

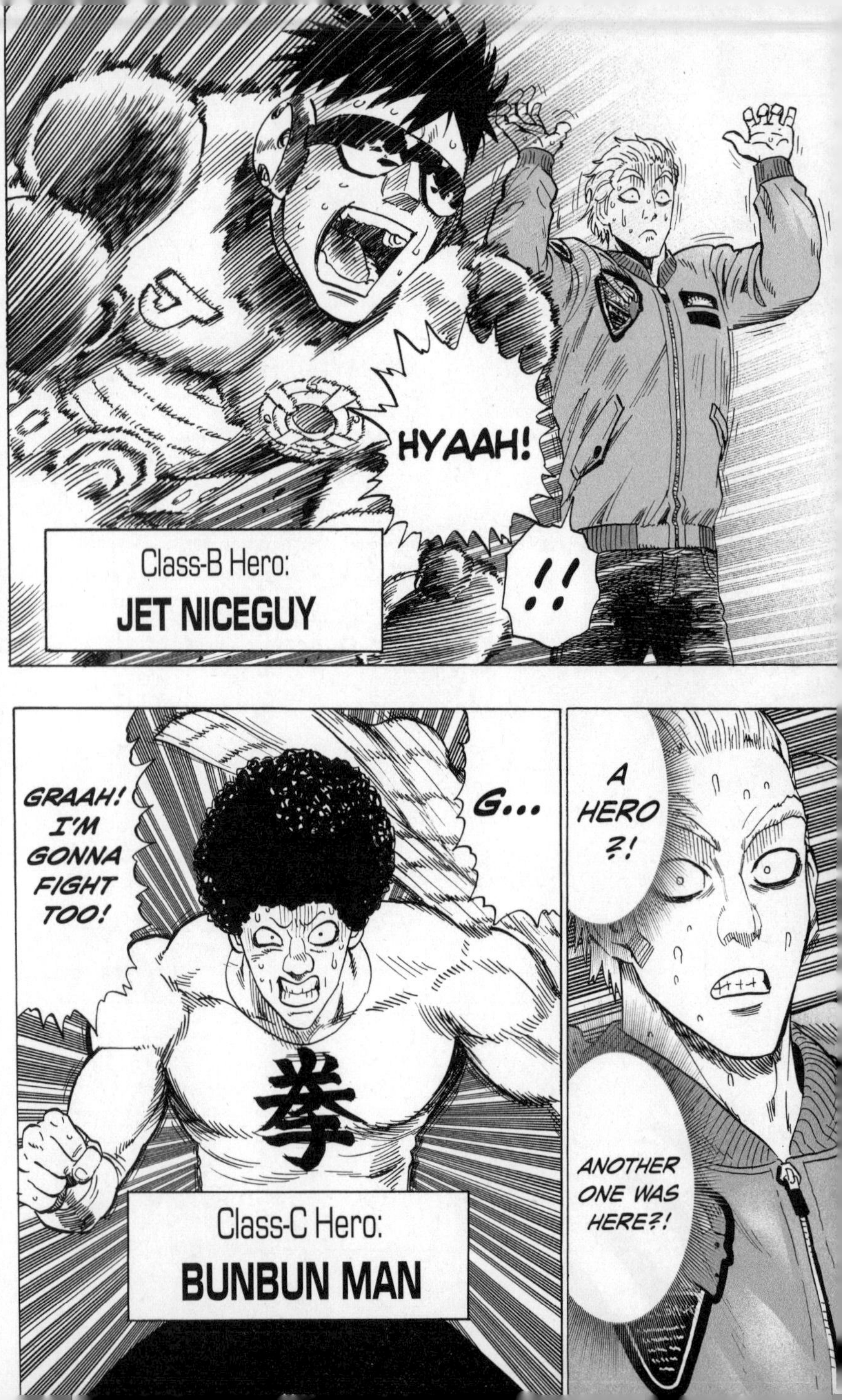

HYAAH!

!!

Class-B Hero:
JET NICEGUY

A HERO ?!

ANOTHER ONE WAS HERE?!

G...

GRAAH! I'M GONNA FIGHT TOO!

Class-C Hero:
BUNBUN MAN

COOL. LET'S WORK TOGETHER.

SWIP

AT RANK 38, I MAY BE AT THE BOTTOM, BUT I'M CLASS A.

Class-A Hero:
"SNAKEBITE FIST" SNEK

LET'S DO THIS!

?
FOUR HEROES WERE HERE?
TWO CLASS C, ONE CLASS B, ONE CLASS A ...
WE CAN DO THIS!
BUT WE ALL EVACUATED ...
YEAH! EVEN I'VE FOUGHT A MONSTER BEFORE!
HEROES?
HEROES ARE HERE?

RAAAAAAAH HEROES!!

YOU'RE CLASS A? WHAT A RELIEF!

WE'RE SAVED!!

YEAH, UH...

PUNCH 26:
UNSTABLE HOPE

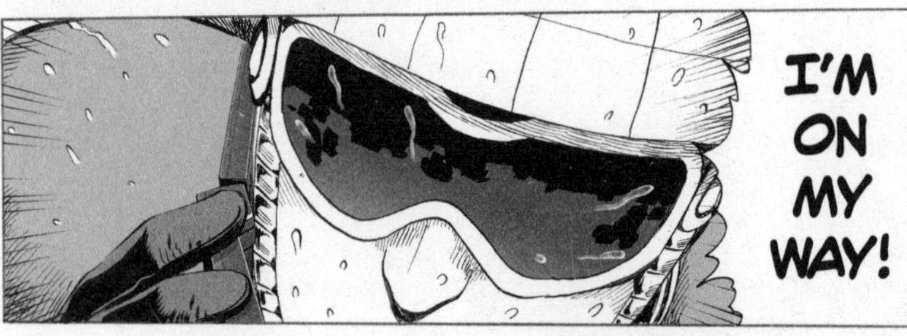

UAAGH! STAND-UP PEDALING MODE!

ROAR, JUS-TICE!!

UAAAGH!

?!

WHOOPS.

SOMEONE DROPPED THEIR PHONE.

HM? IN THE MIDDLE OF A CALL?

HEY! ARE YOU LISTENING, *MUMEN RIDER*?!

YOU'RE ***ABSOLUTELY*** NO MATCH FOR THIS!

YOU MAY BE CLASS C, RANK 1, BUT IT DEFEATED CLASS-S HEROES!

WE'LL ASSEMBLE A TEAM, SO STAY OUT OF THIS!

IT BEAT CLASS-S HEROES?

HUH?! WHO'RE YOU?!

WHERE'S MUMEN RIDER?!

IS THIS THE HERO ASSOCIATION?
YES!
WHO ARE YOU?! PUT MUMEN RIDER ON!

I'M THE HERO SAITAMA.
?!

YOU'RE CLASS C, RANK 2, BUT YOU WANNA FIGHT?!
TELL ME WHERE THE ENEMY IS.

IT'S RAINING, SO HURRY UP.
SAITAMA ...

#0084 GUNMA

#0085

HE SET A BUNCH OF RECORDS IN THE PHYSICAL TESTS...

...AND TOOK OUT THAT METEOR WITH CLASS-S HEROES.

BUT HE DOESN'T HAVE A BACKGROUND IN MARTIAL ARTS OR SPORTS.

HE'S LARGELY UNKNOWN AND THOUGHT TO BE A FRAUD.

I SHOULD KEEP A CLASS-C HERO OUT OF THIS, BUT...

UNDERSTOOD.

GO WHERE I TELL YOU AT ONCE.
MAYBE THIS WILL REVEAL HIS TRUE ABILITY!

BIP

KYAAAH
WAAAAH
EEEEK AAAH
WAAAH
AA...
...RGH!
KYAAAH
EEEEEK

TOSS
IT KILLED JET NICE-GUY!
DON'T FREAK OUT.
WAAH
KYAAAH
HE'S A CYBORG. HE MAY NOT BE DEAD...

HELLLLLLP!
THAT'S WHAT HE GETS FOR RUSHING IN.
I DON'T WANT TO DIE!
AAAA
GO IN ON MY SIGNAL.

ONE...

...TWO...

SHF...

... THR–

PHEW!

I ESCAPED!

SLAM
KRAK
POP POP
SNAP

KRASIISH
?!
TOMP
ARE YOU WITH THE CLAN OF THE SEAFOLK?
I AM HERE TO *ELIMINATE* YOU.
H...

FSSH

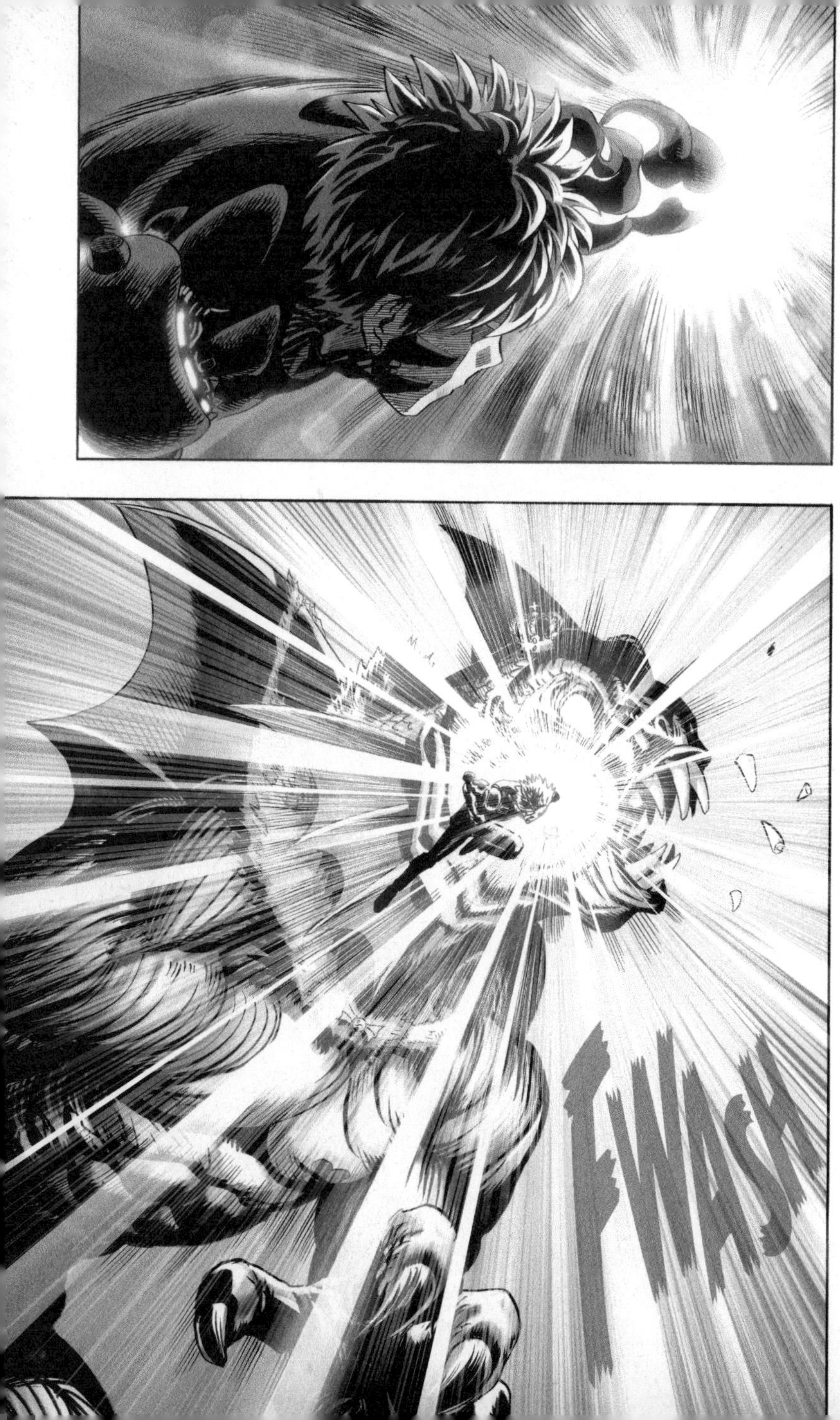

FWASH

BOOM

RRMMM..

HWOOOOOO
WAS THAT ...

...THE LAST ENEMY?

?

CHATTER CHATTER

YA-AA-AA-Y!

COOOL!

RAAAAH

WE'RE SAAA-AAAA-AVED!

WOW!

IT SEEMS LIKE THAT WAS A BIG CRISIS.

SMASH

NOW I'M *MAD*!

SZZZZZZ...
I'M GONNA MESS YOU UP!
I LET MY GUARD DOWN AGAIN.
I NEVER LEARN...

TUMP
I MAY NOT WIN THIS!
ESCAPE FROM THE SHELTER *NOW*!
KLATTER

CRAKL
CRAKL
KLAK
KLAK...
FLEE WHILE I FIGHT HIM!

NOT ONE OF YOUUUUU...
...WILL GET AWAAAY!
CLOMP

WHAK

KA

WHAM
KRAKABAM
WHAMP
BA BABABABABA BABAM

WHOK
THOK
WHAK
BASH
THOK
POW
KLANG
BANG
BANG
BOOM
...

Y...

YOU CAN DO IT, MISTER!!

PTOOEY

SHUT UP.

TIME TO *MELT*, LITTLE GIRL!
WHAT?!

CONTINUED ON PAGE 180...

PUNCH 27:
SHINING IN TATTERS

...
TSHHHHH

AM

YOU COULD HAVE EASILY DODGED THAT ACID...

SPLASH
THUMP
...BUT YOU COMMITTED SUICIDE BY SHIELDING THAT GIRL.
I NEVER CONSIDERED THAT.

YOU'RE DUMB, BUT YOU DID *SLIGHTLY* DAMAGE ME.
I HEALED ALREADY, THOUGH.
TSSSHHHH
WHIRRRRRRRRRRR

DiE.

JUSTICE
CRASH!

I AM THE BICYCLIST FOR JUSTICE ...
... KNOWN AS MUMEN RIDER !!!

THE TOP-RANKING CLASS-C HERO...
NO! DON'T!

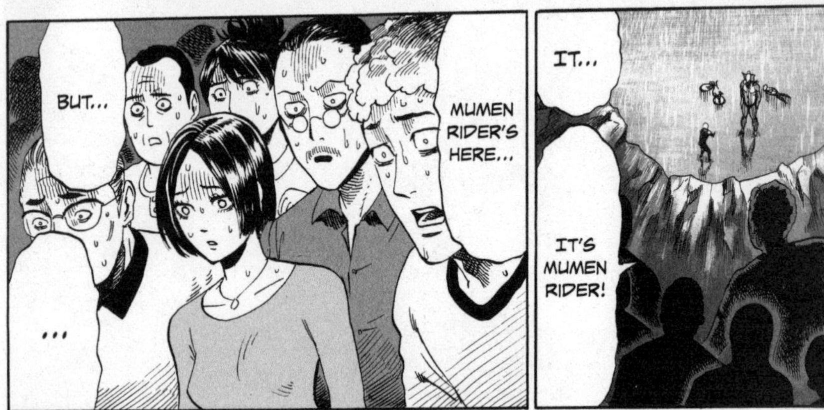

IT...
IT'S MUMEN RIDER!
MUMEN RIDER'S HERE...
BUT...
...

NO MATTER HOW YOU LOOK AT IT...

...A CLASS-C HERO LIKE MUMEN RIDER HAS NO CHANCE OF WINNING!

WHISH

HERE I GO !!

I'M GETTING SICK OF THIS.

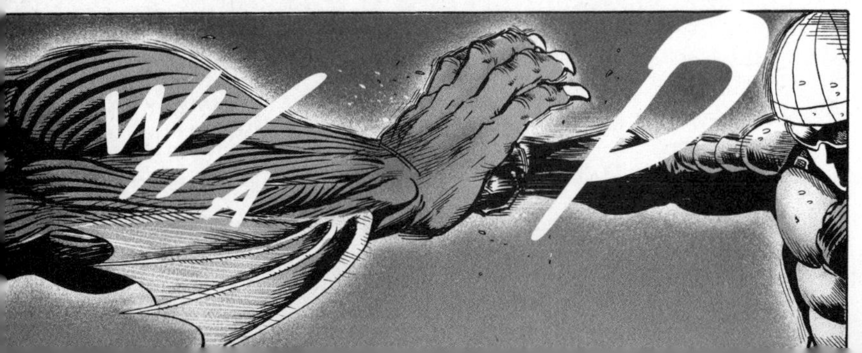

SWSH
SLAM

TOSS

WHAM

OOPS...

...SORRY.

MY KILLING BLOW GOT DELAYED.

URRNGH...
HUH?

UNGH...
I KNOW NO ONE EXPECTS MUCH FROM ME!

WHAM
OOF!

KRS
SHHHHH
AND I KNOW BETTER THAN ANYONE...
...HOW USELESS A CLASS-C HERO IS!

I KNOW...

...I'M TOO WEAK...

...EVEN FOR CLASS B!

WHAT ARE YOU BABBLING ABOUT?
ARE YOU BEGGING FOR YOUR LIFE?

I KNOW MORE THAN ANYONE ELSE...
TOMP

...THAT I'LL NEVER BEAT YOU!!

IT'S NOT ABOUT WINNING OR LOSING!

I JUST HAVE TO STAND HERE AND FACE YOU!

STOP RAMBLING AND JUST DIE ALREADY!

NO MATTER HOW YOU LOOK AT IT, A CLASS-C HERO LIKE MUMEN RIDER HAD NO CHANCE OF WINNING.

BUT...
HANG IN THERE!
YOU CAN DO IT, MUMEN RIDER!
YOU CAN DO IT!
WIN THIS!
MUMEN RIDER!
DO IT FOR US!
GOOD LUCK!
BEAT HIM TO A PULP!
WE CAN COUNT ON YOU!
...THE PEOPLE PLACED THEIR FINAL HOPES IN HIM.

WIN THIS, MUMEN RIDER!

YOU CAN DO IT!

BE CAREFUL OF THAT ACID HE BARFS!

DO YOUR BEST!

I'M A FAN! DON'T DIE!

RRR-RRR-GRA-AAA-AAA-AHH-HHH!

YOU CAN DO IT!
MUMEN RI-
IT'S NO USE. ♥

K
C
H

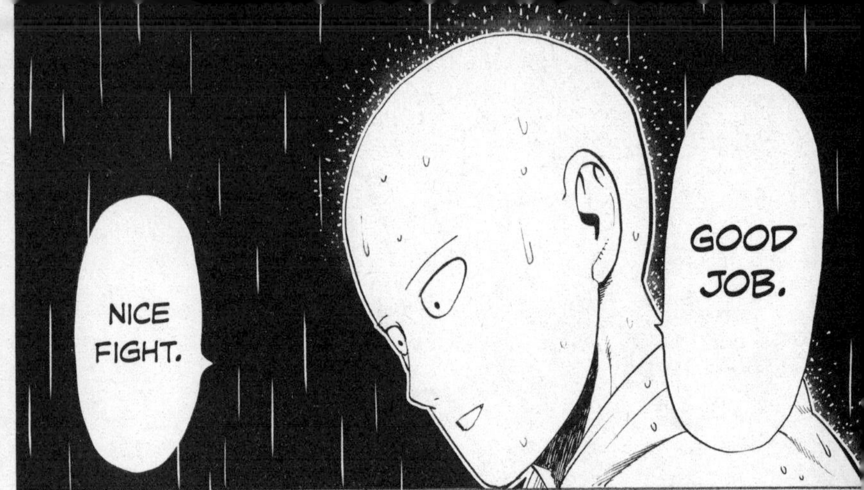
GOOD JOB.
NICE FIGHT.

ANOTHER PARTY CRASHER?

H-HEY, GENOS!
ARE YOU ALIVE ?!
M... MASTER ...
HANG IN THERE FOR A SECOND ...

RMMMN
I'M GONNA GO KILL THIS SEA-FREAK.
I *HEARD* THAT!
KLOK

VEEN

PUNCH 28: IT'S RAINING, SO...

MY BLOW DIDN'T FLATTEN YOU. I'M IMPRESSED.
YOU'RE DIFFERENT FROM THE REST OF THIS TRASH.
NAH...
...YOUR PUNCHES ARE JUST TOO WEAK.

BUT IT LOOKED LIKE THAT MONSTER SMACKED HIM.
...
YOU SURE? THAT MONSTER'S PUNCHES DESTROYED THE OTHER HEROES!
I AM THE DEEP-SEA KING, KING OF THE SEAS.
BULGE
THE SEA IS THE SOURCE OF ALL THINGS, SORT OF LIKE A MOTHER...
PUMP
SO AS THE RULER OF THAT SEA, I STAND ATOP THE PYRAMID OF LIFE!
POP
BUT YOU DEFY ME, SO—
OKAY, FINE...
I HEAR YOU AL-READY.
IT'S RAINING, SO HURRY UP AND FIGHT.

THOK

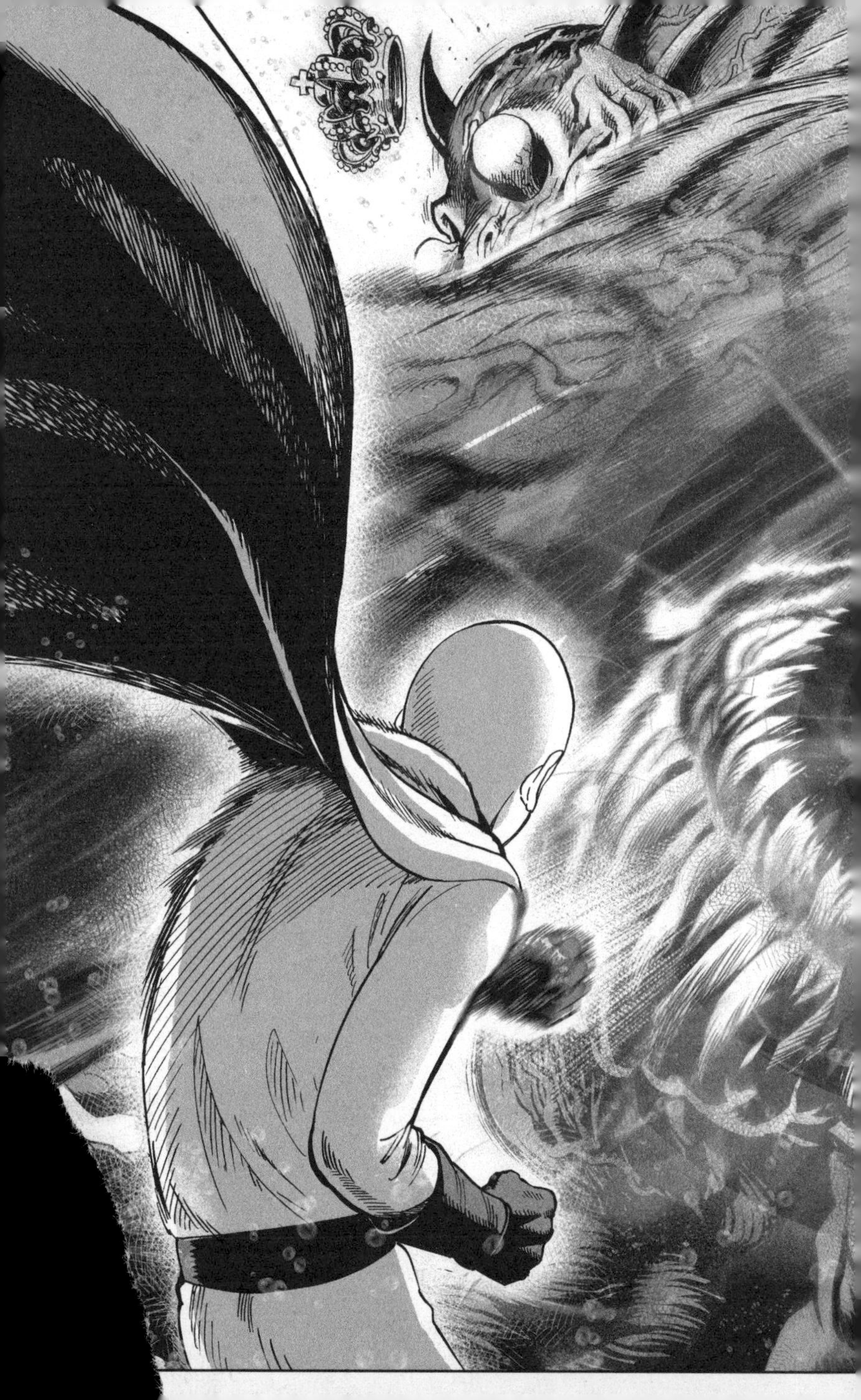

FWUD...

WH T?!
WOW! COOL!
WHO IS THAT?!
WHAT JUST HAP-PENED?!
NO WAY...
HE WON! WE'RE SAAAAVED!!

HE BEAT THE MONSTER WITH ONE BLOW!
IN ONE PUNCH! *ONE PUNCH!*
HOW?! THE OTHER HEROES BARELY SCRATCHED IT!
HE MUST BE SUPER STRONG!!
WE'RE SAVED!
THAT GUY'S IN CLASS C?!
WE'RE STILL ALIVE!

...THAT MONSTER *DID* LOOK WEAK JUST NOW, BUT...

THAT CLASS-C HERO BEAT IT WITH ONE PUNCH! HA HA!

THE HEROES WHO LOST MUST REALLY STINK!

THEY CLAIM TO BE CLASS A AND CLASS S, BUT THERE'S NOTHING TO THEM!

HEY, STOP IT. THEY RISKED THEIR LIVES FOR US.

ANYONE CAN RISK THEIR LIFE!

BUT YOU CAN'T BE A HERO WITHOUT BEATING MONSTERS!

SMIRK

SMIRK

A LOT OF HEROES WERE SERIOUSLY INJURED THIS TIME!

CAN WE REALLY RELY ON THEM NEXT TIME?

NEET

IT WORKED OUT IN THE END...
...BUT IT'S EMBARRASSING WHEN WIMPY HEROES SHOW UP, SO I WISH THEY'D JUST STOP.

THEY CALL THEMSELVES HEROES, SO THEY HAVE TO ACTUALLY HELP US!
HEY!

WHAT'S YOUR PROBLEM?!
WHY'RE YOU GETTING ANGRY?
OUR MONEY IS WHAT FUNDS THE HERO ASSOCIATION! THEY OUGHT TO DO A BETTER JOB!

THAT BALD GUY SOLVED THIS! THE OTHERS JUST DIED NEEDLESSLY!
I SAID STOP IT!

ANYONE COULD BUY SOME TIME! THE OTHER HEROES DIDN'T DO A THING!

BUT WE'RE ALIVE! ISN'T THAT ENOUGH?!

YEAH!

THE OTHER HEROES DIDN'T DO MUCH, BUT IT'S WRONG TO PICK ON THEM!

TSHHHH

HA HA HA HA HA HA HA HA!

WHEW! WHAT A LUCKY BREAK!

THE OTHER HEROES WEAKENED THE MONSTER! SO IT WAS EASY TO BEAT IT!

GOOD THING I WAS LATE! I HARDLY DID ANYTHING! BUT I BEAT IT ALONE!

BUT STILL... ONE PUNCH?
W-WAIT A SECOND...
TH... THAT'S SAITAMA.
HE'S THE ONE THEY SAID WAS A FAKE IN CITY Z!
HUH?! A FAKE?!
WELL, NO ONE'S SURE ABOUT THAT YET.
I'VE HEARD OF HIM TOO. HE SHOWED UP AND IMMEDIATELY STARTED CLIMBING THE RANKS.
THAT'S SUSPICIOUS...
HE JUST SWOOPED IN AT THE END? BUT HIS RANK WILL GO UP?
BUT STILL... ONE PUNCH?!
THE OTHER HEROES WERE GETTING PUMMELED! LIKE THAT NEW GUY GENOS AND MUMEN RIDER WHO LEADS CLASS C!
BUT THIS GUY'S GONNA GET THE CREDIT?
THAT ISN'T FAIR!
BUT MAYBE HE ISN'T REALLY A FAKE...

TEND TO THOSE OTHER HEROES!
IF THEY DIE, I CAN'T USE THEM ANYMORE!
?!

MAYBE HE *IS* A FAKE!
MURMUR
MURMUR
WHOA...
MURMUR
THAT'S NOT FAIR!

BY COMPARISON, THE OTHER HEROES ARE *TRULY HEROIC*!

IF *THEY* HADN'T WEAKENED THE MONSTER, WE'D BE DEAD!
WE SHOULD BE DEEPLY THANKFUL TO THEM!

MASTER SAITAMA...

...IS THIS ALL RIGHT?

IF THIS IS THE PATH YOU CHOOSE TO WALK...

...I WILL NOT INTERFERE.

BUT IF YOU TURN THE PEOPLE AGAINST YOU...
OH...
...WILL YOU BE ABLE TO FUNCTION AS A HERO?
...THE RAIN STOPPED.
THIS WORRIES ME.

BUT IF YOU EVER GET INTO A TIGHT SPOT...

...I WILL BE THERE.

...

I EQUIPPED MYSELF AND HURRIED BACK, BUT...

THAT ROTTEN DEEP SEA KING...
HE MUST HAVE RUN AWAY.

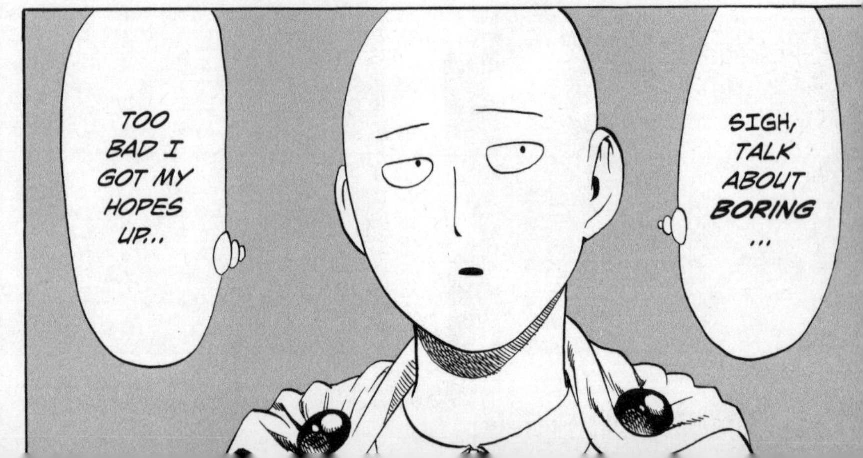

SIGH, TALK ABOUT BORING...
TOO BAD I GOT MY HOPES UP...

GWOOOOOOOO

MADAME SHIBA-BAWA? WHAT IS IT?
IT... IT COMES ...
Great Seer SHIBABAWA

MADAME SHIBA-BAWA?
A STORM OF CALAMITY APPROACHES... AHHH...
MADAME SHIBA-BAWA?
THE ENNNNND NEARSSSS ...
MADAME SHIBA-BAWA! TAKE HOLD OF YOUR-SELF!

HUFF
HUFF
THE EARTH IS IN DANGER!

PUNCH 29: CLASS B

WHAT'S THIS?

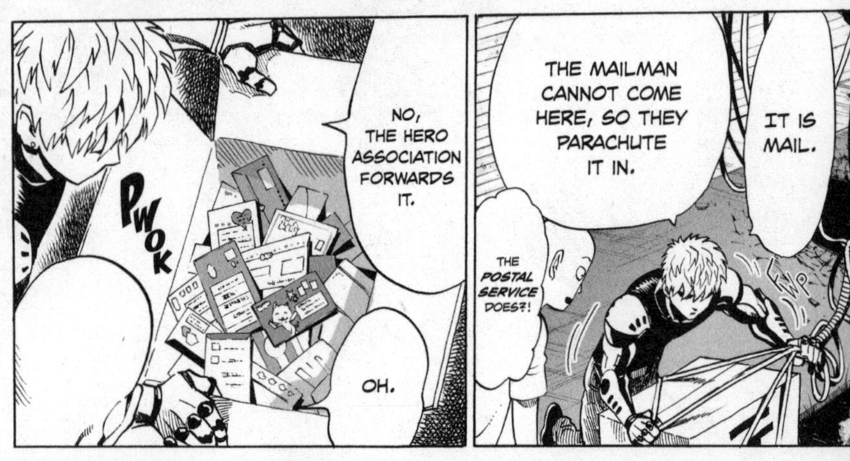
IT IS MAIL.
THE MAILMAN CANNOT COME HERE, SO THEY PARACHUTE IT IN.
THE *POSTAL SERVICE* DOES?!
NO, THE HERO ASSOCIATION FORWARDS IT.
PWOK
OH.

THEY ARE FROM ORDINARY PEOPLE.
MOSTLY FAN LETTERS.
REALLY?
HEY! SOME ARE FOR ME!!!
Class-C Hero Saitama

LET'S HURRY HOME AND OPEN THEM!
THERE ARE FIVE FOR YOU, MASTER...
C'MON, HURRY IT UP!!

DUMP

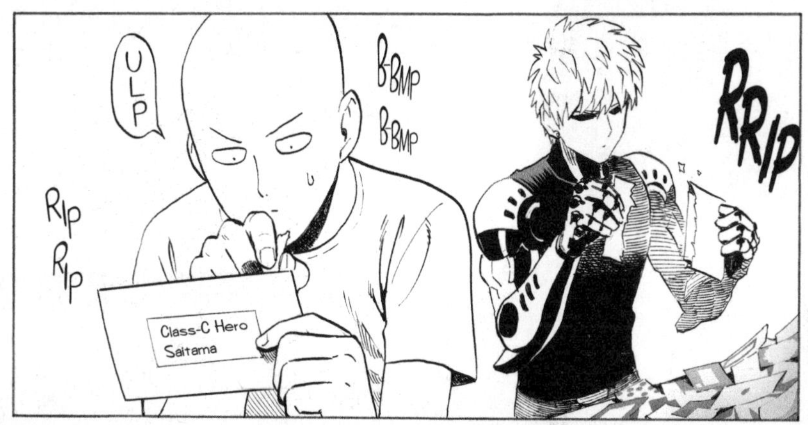
RRIP
B-BMP
B-BMP
ULP
RIP
RIP
Class-C Hero
Saitama

Dear Genos,
I'm a big fan!! I've been
cheering for you ever
since the first time I
saw you! I think you are
a true hero. I'm even in
your fan club!! I'm really
crazy about you and

...

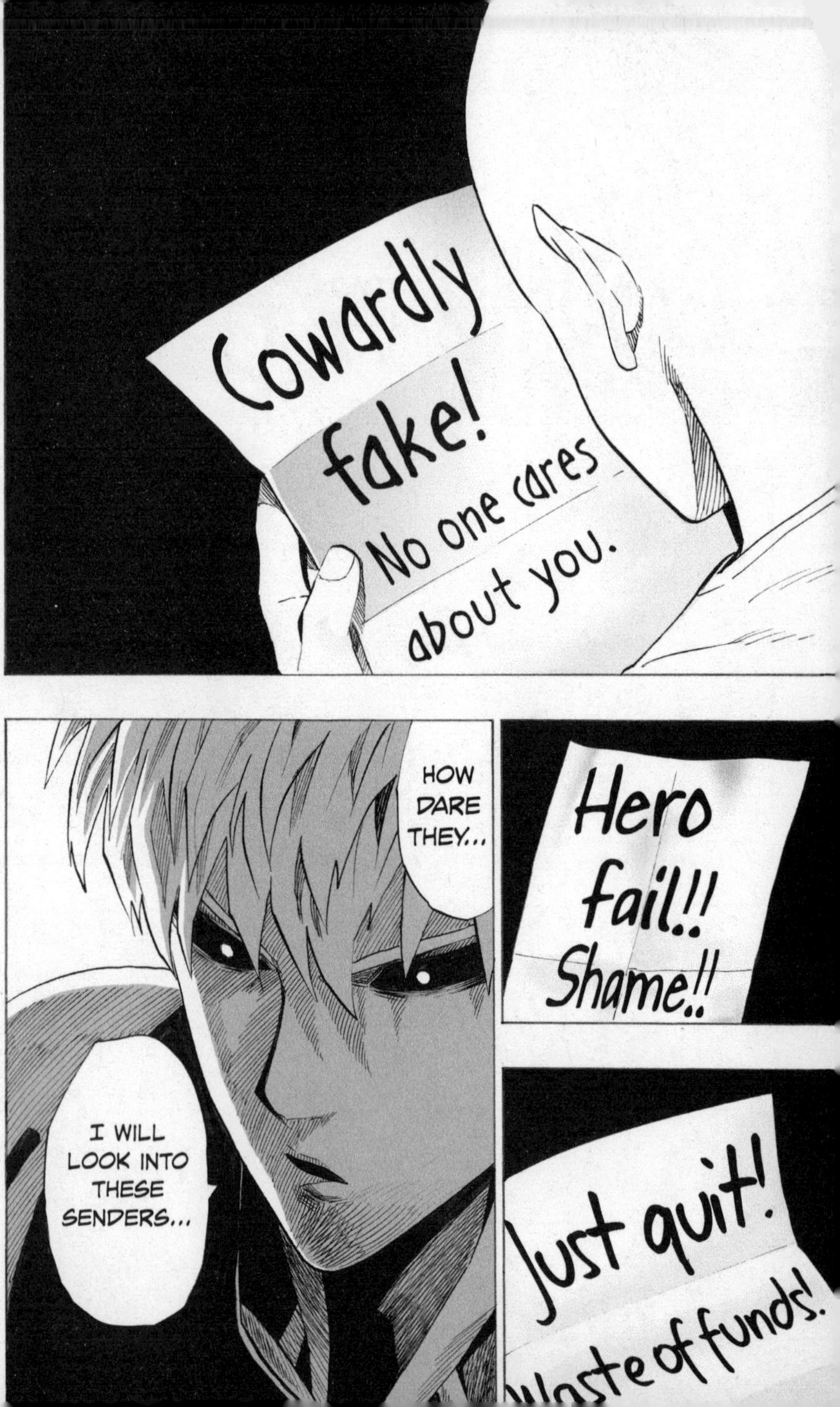

Cowardly fake! No one cares about you.

Hero fail!! Shame!!

Just quit! Waste of funds!

DON'T THEY HAVE ANYTHING BETTER TO DO?

...
OH...

...HERE'S ANOTHER ONE.
FWIP
Class-C Hero Saitama

I SHOULD NOT HAVE SHOWN HIM.
RUSTLE
RUSTLE
THIS IS MY FAULT...

...

To the hero Saitama,

~~Thanks to you I~~

Thank you!!

AN ACQUAINTANCE?
I DUNNO. BUT HE'S THANKING ME.
YOU MUST HAVE HELPED HIM SOMETIME.
?

WHAT'S THAT ONE?
THIS IS FROM THE HERO ASSOCIATION.
IT IS FOR YOU.
ARE THEY FIRING ME?
OH WELL.
HUH?
Certificate of Prom
CLASS C
RANK 1
Saitam
(Hero name:
WHAT IS THIS?
CLASS C...
RANK 1
Saitama
(Hero name: no
RANK 1...

HERO ASSOCIATION: BRANCH Z

WHEN YOU JOINED THE REGISTRY, YOU RECEIVED A MANUAL.
HAVEN'T YOU READ IT?
IT CONTAINS THE RULES OF THE ASSOCIATION.
I COULD PROBABLY FIND IT IF I LOOKED.
ARE YOU GONNA CHEW ME OUT?

NO.
CONGRATULATIONS ON ADVANCING TO CLASS C, RANK 1.

OH, ARE YOU THE GUYS...
...WHO RATE THE HEROES?

THE REVIEW BOARD IS QUITE LARGE...
...BUT WE FOUR WILL HANDLE YOUR INTER-VIEW.
INTER-VIEW?

WE CAN GRANT YOU ENTRANCE TO CLASS B.
OF COURSE, YOU MAY STAY IN CLASS C IF YOU WANT.

WOULD YOU *LIKE* TO JOIN CLASS B?
IT WOULD MEAN STARTING IN THE BOTTOM RANK.

AND WITH GENOS IN CLASS S...

...I CAN'T STAY IN CLASS C FOREVER...

AND HAVE A SEAT.

YOU WANNA KNOW MY MOTIVATION AND STUFF?

SO THAT'S SAITAMA...

HE SET AN OVERALL RECORD ON THE PHYSICAL EXAM, BUT...
SOME SAY HE CHEATED ON THAT.

CHEW CHEW
"HE PLANTED A RIGGED STOPWATCH."
"HE BRIBED THE OFFICIALS."
"HE FORCED THE OTHER CANDIDATES TO BACK OUT."
AND SO ON...
HIS RESULTS ARE THE SUBJECT OF GREAT DOUBT.

BUT ISN'T IT TOO LATE FOR THAT?
WE SHOULD LET HIM ADVANCE AND OBSERVE HIM.
IF HE'S REAL, HE CAN HANDLE CLASS B.

BUT IF HE'S A FAKE...
...HE'LL *REGRET* IT.

HE'LL ALREADY HAVE STEPPED INTO AN UNFORGIVING WORLD.

CLASS B? DON'T BOTHER ME WITH THAT!
WHO CARES ABOUT THE BOTTOM CLASSES?
Class-A, Rank-1 Hero
Amai Mask, a.k.a. Handsome Kamen
WELL, THE BOARD OF DIRECTORS DECIDED...
...THAT TO GARNER PUBLIC SUPPORT...
...YOU WOULD ADVISE IN MATTERS OF THIS SORT.
I ONLY ASKED FOR INPUT ON CLASSES A AND HIGHER BECAUSE OF THEIR SOCIAL IMPACT.
WE CAN'T HAVE THEM STIRRING UP TROUBLE.

BUT ALL RIGHT. I'LL DO IT.
HIS NAME IS SAITAMA. NO HERO NAME.

HE CERTAINLY HAS A CLASS-C OR B AURA...
BUT AS LONG AS HE DOESN'T RAISE A SCANDAL...
FINE. *PROMOTE HIM.*

PACHINKO JUMBO SLOT
P

MAN, THAT TOOK FOREVER!
BUT I WASN'T BUSY, SO...
TUMP
TUMP

Certificate of Promotion
CLASS B
RANK 101
Saitama
(Hero name: none)
NOW I'M IN CLASS B.

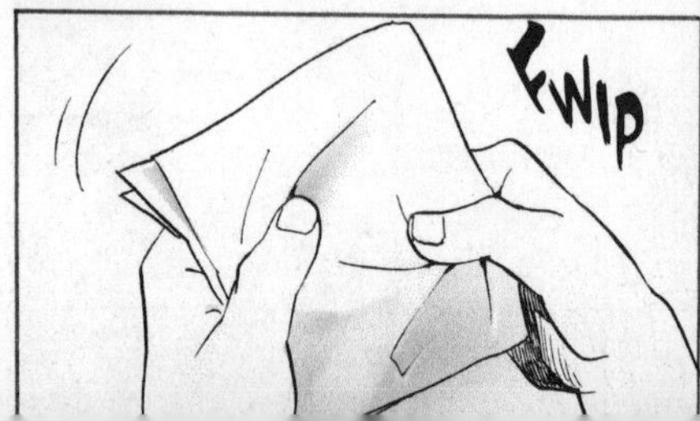
FWIP

HEY...

SHF

...THAT SMELLS GOOD.

I'VE BEEN LOOKING FOR YOU.

I COULDN'T EXPRESS EVERYTHING IN MY *LETTER*.

OH HEY. IT'S YOU...
FROM BEFORE...

OKAY, I'LL HAVE *MOZUKU* SEAWEED!
CHEF! YOUR FINEST MOZUKU!

THIS MOVEMENT MUST CONTAIN THE SECRET TO STRENGTH!!
LIKE THIS ?!
SNAP
WHAT ARE YOU DOING ...?

BONUS MANGA: WHAT CAN'T BE BOUGHT

TWENTY YEN.

HUH?

YOUR ACCOUNT HAS A BALANCE OF TWENTY YEN.

ABC BANK

IT HAS BEEN INACTIVE FOR QUITE SOME TIME.

OH... RIGHT.

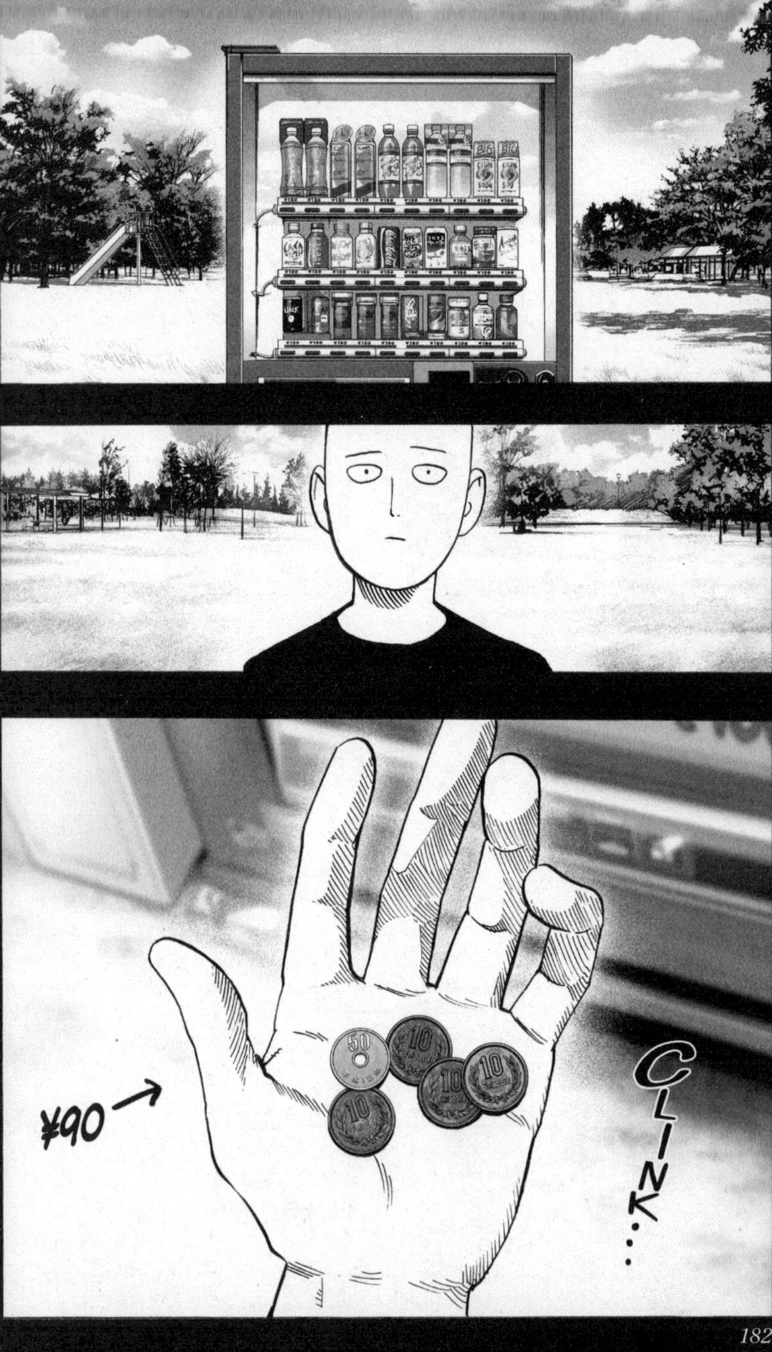
¥90
CLINK...

あずき
ゼリーサイダー
¥120
¥120
つめた〜い
...
COFFEE
BOSA
I SHOULDN'T BE DISAPPOINTED.
I'M SURE IT TASTES BAD.

CLINK
CLANK
WHOA!! WHAT'S THE CORPSE OF A DANGEROUS CREATURE DOING OUT HERE?!
OH NO! WE SHOULD BLOCK IT OFF SO PEOPLE CAN'T GET CLOSE AND TOUCH IT.
IT COULD BE POISONOUS.

KEEP OUT KEEP OUT KEEP OUT KEEP OUT KEEP OUT
KEEP OUT KEEP OUT
PAT
WHEW!
LIKE THAT!
PAT
OOH, LOOK! IT'S THE HERO D-PAD!!
YOU'RE RIGHT!! COOL!
LOOK OVER HERE, D-PAD!
KEEP OUT KEEP OUT
WE DID GOOD WORK.
YES.
THE CHILDREN LOVE YOU.
IT'S LIKE WE'RE THE ONES WHO DEFEATED IT...
Class C, Rank 25
D-PAD
Class C, Rank 44
FUNERAL SUSPENDERS

あずき
ゼリー
サイダー
¥120
¥12
20
つめた〜い
BEEP
KLANK
WHAT IS THAT? DOES IT TASTE GOOD?
I'LL KNOW WHEN I DRINK IT!
SHAKE
SHAKE
GULP
GULP
WHIP
THREE POINTS!!

The Hero Association's compensation system is clear and simple.
It pays at the end of each month based on rank.

The Hero Ranking is based on points earned for heroic deeds...
The board considers eyewitness accounts and reports by the heroes themselves...
...but the criteria are known only to the assessment board.
...but results are often not reflected in the order.

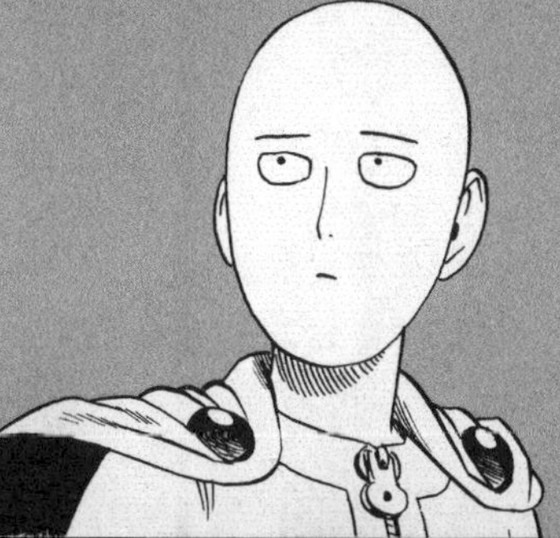
However, few heroes express dissatisfaction because it would make a poor impression.
The Hero Association is supposed to be a nonprofit organization dedicated to justice and compassion.

So while Class-C heroes receive low pay, they cannot complain.

KLONK

CLANK

ROLL ROLL...

MY RANK MIGHT GO UP.

I CAN FEEL A PROMOTION TO CLASS B COMING.

LET THE ASSOCIATION DISPOSE OF THE BODY.
SHALL WE CONTINUE ON PATROL?
YES.
TUG

STARE—
YEAH... IT LOOKS AWFUL.
CLUNK
But that isn't why Saitama is broke.

I NEED TEN YEN.
HUH?
FOR ADZU-
GRAAAAH!!!
EVERY-ONE GET DOWN!!
WHAM
GET OUT THE MONEY!!
EEK!
WHAM

PACK THE MONEY INTO THESE FOUR BAGS!

YOU CUSTOMERS DON'T MOVE!

Wanted Man, Class A

BULL-BULL

GATHER THE DOUGH AND LET'S SPLIT!
MA-MAAA!
THEY TOOK A BOY HOSTAGE ...
OH NO ...
HOW TERRIBLE!

WAIT!!

THE HEROES ...
... D-PAD ...
... AND ...
... FUNERAL SUSPENDERS ...
...ARE HERE!

GOOD THING WE CHANCED ALONG!
THIS IS AWESOME!
SSNAAAAPP
WE WON'T LET YOU GET AWAY!

GAH!
SWS
VWSH
?!

WHOK
TATATATA TUMP
!
LOOK OUT BEHIND YOU, DUMMY!!
HRAH!
BASH

WHSH

HWAH!

UGH!!

WHUD

WHACK
WHACK
WHACK
WHACK
WHACK
WHACK
WHACK
WHACK
WHACK
!!

BAM
GAH ?!!

A CLASS-C HERO IS NO MATCH FOR A MAN WITH AN A-CLASS BOUNTY ON HIS HEAD...
...PIP-SQUEAK.

LET'S GO.
SHUMP

MAMAAAA!!

NOOO! MY SON!!!

SOME-ONE! ANYONE! HELP MY BOY!!

UH-OH ...

SCREEEEEECH

13-13

IT WENT WELL AGAIN.
OF COURSE IT DID.
WEEOO
WEEOO
MR. BULL-BULL? WHAT ABOUT THE KID?

UH... WHUH?
THE WHEEL ...
HEY! WHY'RE YOU HEADING INTO TOWN?!
HEY!!
VWOOSH

WHAT THE HECK?

STEP ON THE BRAKES!!

IT WON'T STOP!!

A MOVIE SHOOT?

KAWHOMP
TOSS

FWSH
しょう油
I DON'T KNOW WHAT'S GOING ON...

KCHAK
CLOMP
CLOMP

PAT
PAT

...BUT DID YOU DO THIS?

MY MONEY WAS IN THAT BANK.

I CAN'T LET YOU HAVE IT.

DIE!

FUMP
FUMP

IT'S ALL BUNDLES OF BILLS ...
...

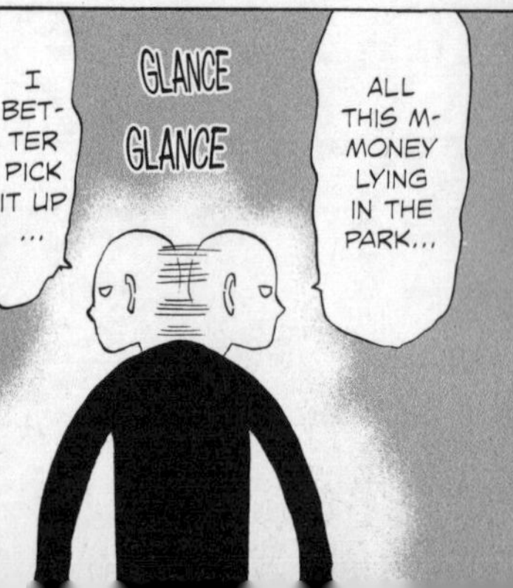

ALL THIS M-MONEY LYING IN THE PARK...
GLANCE
GLANCE
I BET-TER PICK IT UP ...

...

THANKS, OLD GUY!

THANK YOU!
GAH

Y-YEAH ...
YOU ALL RIGHT?
YEP!
I'M FINE!

MOM SAID I SHOULD THANK PEOPLE WHO HELP ME!

THIS IS ALL I HAVE...
CLINK
...BUT ADULTS LIKE MONEY, RIGHT?

YOU CAN HAVE MY ALLOW-ANCE!
THANK YOU!!

PAT
I GRATEFULLY ACCEPT...
...AND RETURN IT TO YOU.
USE IT FOR SOMETHING MORE IMPORTANT.

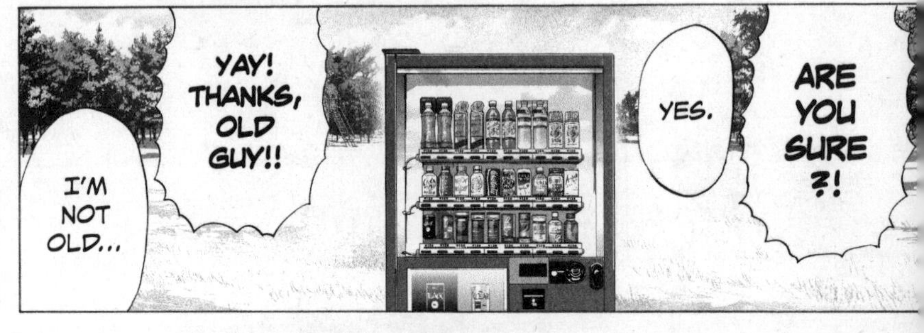

ARE YOU SURE?!
YES.
YAY! THANKS, OLD GUY!!
I'M NOT OLD...

THAT'S WHAT HAPPENED.
BUT DO I REALLY LOOK THAT POOR?
しょう油

NO, NOT... THAT'S NOT...
NOT THAT... YES... WELL...
UH... THAT REMINDS ME...

IT TASTES... DISGUSTING ...

THE EXPIRATION DATE IS IN TWO YEARS, SO WE HAVE WORK TO DO.

EVEN WITH MONEY, NOTHING CHANGES...

5 Shining in Tatters (End)

BONUS

OH! MUMEN!
SKRK
HEY! IT'S SAITAMA!
ON PATROL?
GOOD WORK.
IT'S NOTHING.
I LIKE DOING IT.
THIRSTY?
YEAH! I'M PARCHED.
YOU'RE JUST IN TIME, THEN.
The pedals had never felt so heavy before.

ONE-PUNCH MAN 5

THE "ONE PUNCH"... MUST START. MUST DOWN. MUST END. THE HERO IS CALLED "ONE PUNCH MAN."

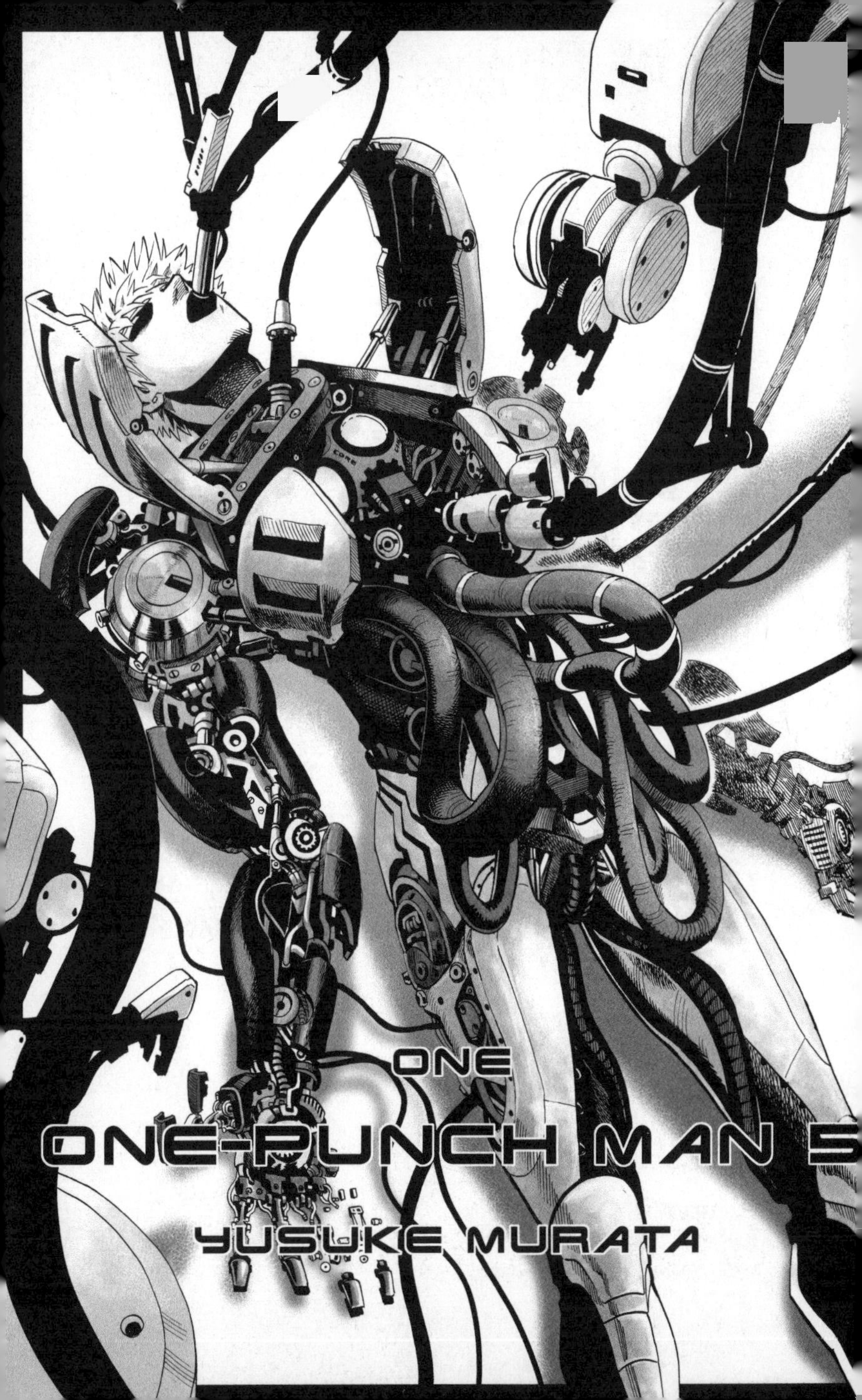
ONE
ONE-PUNCH MAN 5
YUSUKE MURATA

END NOTES

PAGE 63, PANELS 2 & 3:

The boy's shirt says "brat," and the man's shirt says "old man."

PAGE 70, PANEL 3:

The kanji on Bunbun Man's shirt means "fist."

PAGE 183, PANEL 1:

The drink in the vending machine is Adzuki Jelly Cider.

PAGE 186, PANEL 4:

Saitama's shirt says "soy sauce."

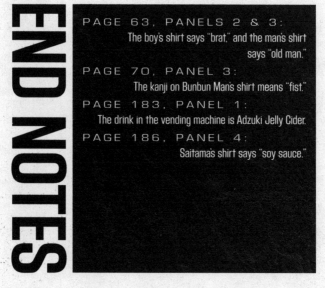

ONE-PUNCH MAN

VOLUME 5

SHONEN JUMP MANGA EDITION

STORY BY | ONE
ART BY | YUSUKE MURATA

TRANSLATION | JOHN WERRY
TOUCH-UP ART AND LETTERING | JAMES GAUBATZ
DESIGN | FAWN LAU
SHONEN JUMP SERIES EDITOR | JOHN BAE
GRAPHIC NOVEL EDITOR | JENNIFER LEBLANC

First published in Japan in 2012 by SHUEISHA Inc., Tokyo.
English translation rights arranged by SHUEISHA Inc.

Printed in the U.S.A.

Published by VIZ Media, LLC
P.O. Box 77010
San Francisco, CA 94107

viz.com

10 9 8 7 6 5 4 3
First printing, March 2016
Third printing, July 2018

SHONEN JUMP
shonenjump.com

PARENTAL ADVISORY
ONE-PUNCH MAN is rated T for Teen and is recommended for ages 13 and up. This volume contains realistic and fantasy violence.

STOP!

YOU'RE READING THE WRONG WAY!

★ **ONE-PUNCH MAN** READS FROM **RIGHT TO LEFT**, STARTING IN THE UPPER-RIGHT CORNER. JAPANESE IS READ FROM RIGHT TO LEFT, MEANING THAT ACTION, SOUND EFFECTS, AND WORD-BALLOON ORDER ARE COMPLETELY REVERSED FROM ENGLISH ORDER.

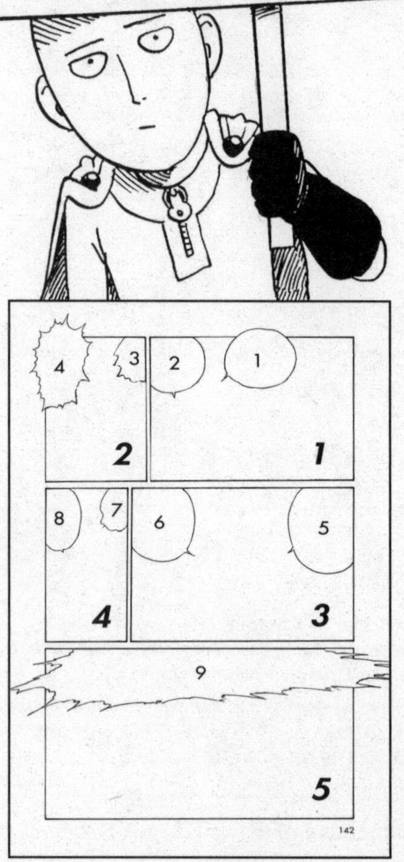